JAVA Interview Questions

SAPCOOKBOOK.COM

TABLE OF CONTENTS

Java Interview Questions

SAPCOOKBOOK
Equity Press

☞ QUESTION 1

Thread to enter synchronized function

If a class has two synchronized functions, a thread enters one of the synchronized functions, and then is it possible for another thread to enter the second synchronized function?

✍ ANSWER

The thread can enter into the other synchronized methods if the other method is static synchronized method while the first method is non static synchronized method. This is because in order to enter into the synchronized method the thread should acquire a lock. If it is a static synchronized method then the thread requires a class level lock or else it requires an instance level lock.

☞ QUESTION 2

Repeated Patterns

How to check for repeated patterns in a password?

✍ ANSWER

By using JavaScript we can break a string into small substring and compare each sub string.

☞ QUESTION 3

Static Members

Can we serialize the static members?

✍ ANSWER

Yes, you can serialize the Static data also. For this use the Externalizable tagged interface and use writeObject() is. Otherwise if we implement the Serializable interface and serialize the data then static variable value will be stored as zero. So instead of this we use Externalizable interface.

☞ QUESTION 4

Hiding and Overriding

What is the difference between hiding & overriding?

✍ ANSWER

Overloading is related to one particular class. If we define two methods in the same class with same name, but different input parameters, then it is called overloading. Overriding is related to super and sub class. He you define a method with same name, accepting the same parameter as that of your super class. Then the method in the sub class is said to override the method in the super class.

☞ QUESTION 5

Hashtable( )

What is the capacity of Hashtable()?

✍ ANSWER

The initial size of the hashtable is 11. The load factor is 0.75. If it reaches the bound (i.e. 11*0.75=8) then it's doubled size is 16. It keeps on increasing its size up to the maximum RAM size.

☞ QUESTION 6

Operator overloading

Why operator overloading is not allowed in Java?

✍ ANSWER

By using the operator overload, you will have lots of problems there. Sometimes even the programmer gets confused. It increases the complexity of the program. For this reason, the functionality was removed in Java.

☞ QUESTION 7

Significance of null interface

What is the significance of null interface in Java?

✍ ANSWER

We define this as a mark up interface. We use this interface because it should be recognized by Java Virtual Machine in order to make the objects selected for network be enabled and serialized. It should also be able to select particular objects to be participated by users in a Client/server Communication environment.

☞ QUESTION 8

Definition of length

I can get the size (length) of any array (let a[]) by a.length.

What does this "length" word actually signify? Where is it defined in Java and what is its actual definition?

✍ ANSWER

Length gives the current length of an array a[] while it is not null. Size gives its capacity.

☞ **QUESTION 9**

Java types

Name the eight primitive Java type.

✍ **ANSWER**

These are as follows:

1) Boolean

2) int

3) float

4) byte

5) short

6) char

7) long

8) double

☞ **QUESTION 10**

Native Methods and other approaches

What are the traverses in a binary tree?
Write down how you will create a Binary tree?
What is a constructor and virtual function? Can we call a virtual function in a constructor? Give examples.

✍ **ANSWER**

In applet we use native methods that won't look good. With that, the Sun Micro Systems people invented javax.swing class wherein Japplet will provide a better look and feel than applet.

The native methods are written in c-language where Japplet is written in Java only.

At the time of release they didn't complete the entire coding part of java.awt. That's why they used c-language and they developed awt-based on c-language. Later on they developed the use of swings.

☞ QUESTION 11

Cloneable Interface

What is Cloneable Interface in Java? Is it implemented by the Prototype Design Pattern?

✍ ANSWER

The cloneable interface is provided by Java for the classes that want to support the function clone or want to override it.

This function is supposed to create and return the copy of an object.

☞ QUESTION 12

Java Pointer

Does Java have a pointer?

✍ ANSWER

No. Java does not have a pointer but we can use the new operator.

For example:

The name of the method is firstname;

we can create an object as:

firstname f=new firstname;

This allocates the memory according to the size of the method firstname.

.

☞ QUESTION 13

Retrieving images from MS Word

How do you retrieve images from an MS Word document using Java.

✍ ANSWER

You can apply the following:

Export the ASP page to a Word document. There is a way to direct the html produced from an ASP page to Word document instead of displaying it in a standard browser and in order to do that you have to change the content type of the server response. Put the following line on the top of your ASP page:

"<% Response.ContentType = "applica";

☞ QUESTION 14

Calling a COM object

How to call a COM object within Java?

✍ ANSWER

The Java library allows Java applications to seamlessly interoperate with the Microsoft Component Object Model.

First, generate Java type definitions from a COM type library.

Here we are doing for the type library the Windows Scripting Host:

> java -jar tlbimp.jar -o wsh -p test.wsh %WINDIR%\system32\ wshom.ocx

Then we are able to call WSH objects/methods. public class Main

```
{
  public static void main(String[] args) {
    IFileSystem3 fs = ClassFactory.createFileSystemObject();
    for( String file : args )
      System.out.println(fs.getFileVersion(file));
}
```

☞ **QUESTION 15**

Serialization

Why do we need to serialize the object?

✍ **ANSWER**

Serialization means "to convert into byte stream". We need to serialize the object so that if many thread calls that function then consistency should be maintained.

☞ QUESTION 16

Printing query

Imagine there is a class Employee. We create an object of Employee:

Employee a= New Employee();
If we are giving
System.out.println(a);

What gets printed?

✍ ANSWER

The command gives the classname and the memory location. For example: Employee@187c6c7 where 187c6c7 is the memory location. From there, you can determine what gets printed.

☞ QUESTION 17

Link list

How linklist can be implemented in Java with out using the collection framework?

✍ ANSWER

Java(tm) has no user-visible pointers, so how would you do a linked list? Each element needs to point to the next one, doesn't it?

Fortunately there is a way, illustrated using this brief example:

```
// source file link.java     public class link {          public
int value;          // value of element          public link next;
// reference to next          // constructor          public
link(int n, link ln)          {                    value = n;
next = ln;          }          public static void main(String args[])
{          // initialize list head          link head =
null;          // add some entries to list          for
(int i = 1; i <= 10; i++)          head = ncw link(i,
head);          // dump out entries          link p =
head;          while (p != null) {          System.
out.println(p.value);          p = p.next;          }
}     }Java does not have pointers, but instead uses implicit
references. A line like:
```

link next;does not actually declare an object instance of

class link, but rather a reference to an object instance. The line:

head = new link(i, head);creates a new element for the list, sets its value, and then sets the object reference in "next" to point at the old list head (this approach means that the last element inserted will be at the head of the list). Saying:

p = p.next;simply picks up the "next" reference from the current node and makes it the current element being worked on.

When we're done using this list, we can simply leave the list with all its elements lying around - garbage collection will eventually reclaim it.

If what you really want to do in a Java application is manage a list of numbers, there are higher-level techniques in the language and library (such as the Vector class) for doing so more cleanly than the approach illustrated here. This example shows some of what can be done underneath to implement the higher-level schemes.

☞ QUESTION 18

A protable JDBC connection

How do you make JDBC connection a protable without specific drivers?

✍ ANSWER

JDBC can't do its job without a driver, and the JDBC management layer must know the location of each and every database driver available to it. There are two ways that JDBC does this. First, upon initialization, the java.sql. DriverManager class searches for the sql.drivers property in the system's properties. If it exists, the DriverManager class will load it. Second, you can call the specific driver explicitly, thus avoiding the search. Drivers may be downloaded over the network (Internet or Intranet) as an option.

```
import java.net.URL;
import java.sql.*;

class Select {

public static void main(String argv[]) {
try {
// Create a URL specifying an ODBC data source name.
String url = "jdbc:odbc:wombat";

// Connect to the database at that URL.
Connection con = DriverManager.getConnection(url, "kgh",
"");
```

```
// Execute a SELECT statement
Statement stmt = con.createStatement();
ResultSet rs = stmt.executeQuery("SELECT a, b, c, d, key
FROM Table1");

// Step through the result rows.
System.out.println("Got results:");
while (rs.next()) {
// get the values from the current row: int a = rs.getInt(1);
Numeric b = rs.getNumeric(2);
char c[] = rs.getString(3).tocharArray();
boolean d = rs.getBoolean(4);
String key = rs.getString(5);

// Now print out the results:
System.out.print(" key=" + key);
System.out.print(" a-" + a);
System.out.print(" b=" + b);
System.out.print(" c=");
for (int I = 0; I < c.lngth; I++) {
System.out.print(c[i]);
}
System.out.print(" d=" + d);
System.out.print("\n");
}

stmt.close();
con.close();

} catch (java.lang.Exception ex) {
ex.printStackTrace();
```

☞ QUESTION 19

Multi-threading and multi-processing

What is the difference between multi-threading and multi-processing?

✍ ANSWER

Multi-threading is when we can open multiple pages whenever we like but we cannot process data one at a time.

Multi-processing is when we can do or process different pages at a time. While one page is being accessed we can process other pages also.

☞ QUESTION 20

Java Memory Model

Can you explain what is a Java Memory Model?

✍ ANSWER

The Java Memory Model allows the compiler and cache to take significant liberties with the order in which data is moved between a processor-specific cache/register and main memory, unless the programmer has explicitly asked for certain visibility guarantees being synchronized or volatile. This means that in the absence of synchronization, memory operations can appear to happen in different orders from the perspective of different threads. A class defined without any synchronization: final class check1{ private int a = 0; private long b = 0; void set() { a = 1; b = -1; } Boolean check() { return ((b == 0) || (b == -1 && a == 1)); }};

☞ QUESTION 21

Creating an object

If I create an object which is to be serialized do I need to implement any methods?

✍ ANSWER

You just need to implement the Interface Serializable and don't have to implements any methods. This is because Serializable Interface has no methods. It's just a Marker/Tag Interface which tells that this object is serializable.

☞ QUESTION 22

equals( ) method and ==

What is the difference between equals() method and == ?

✍ ANSWER

The == operator checks to see if two objects are exactly the same object. Two strings may be different objects, but have the same value. The .equals() method is used to compare strings for equality(content).

☞ QUESTION 23

Throw and throws clause

What is the difference between throw and throws clause? Explain in programmatically defined terms.

✍ ANSWER

Throw is used to throw an exception manually, whereas throws clause is used in the case of checked exceptions, to re-intimate the compiler that has handled the exception. So in effect, throws is to be used at the time of defining a method and also at the time of calling that function, when raising a checked exception.

To programmatically explain the difference between throw and throws clause:

```
class MyException extends Exception //to create our own exception
{
public String toString()   //overriding the method toString()
to print the desired msg.
{
return "Can not divide a no. with one: "+"MyException";
}
public static void main(String args[]) throws MyException
//use of throws
{
int a=Integer.parseInt(args[0]);
int b=Integer.parseInt(args[1]);
if(b==1)
```

throw new MyException(); // rises an MyException, if we try
to divide a no. with 1
else
System.out.println((float)a/b);
}
}

If we want to raise our own exception, we have to use either
throws or to handle the exception by try-catch. If not, it gives
the compile time error.

And throw is to raise the exception manually; in the above
program I raised an exception when you try to divide a
number with 1. (Own Exception)

☞ QUESTION 24

The singleton design pattern

Answer the following questions referring to the singleton design pattern:

1. Explain singleton pattern in Java?
2. Explain up casting and down casting?
3. How do you code a singleton in Java?
4. How do you read XML file in Java?
5. Give an example of the Decorator pattern in the Java API.
6. What are the services provided by the container?
7. What are bean managed transaction?
8. What are transaction attributes?
9. What is JTS?

✍ ANSWER

The singleton design pattern is designed to restrict instantiation of a class to one (or a few) objects. This is useful when exactly one object is needed to coordinate actions across the system. Sometimes it is generalized to systems that operate more efficiently when only one or a few objects exist.

The singleton pattern is implemented by creating a class with a method that creates a new instance of the object if one does not exist. If one does exist it returns a reference to the object that already exists. To make sure that the object cannot be instantiated any other way the constructor is made either private or protected.

The singleton pattern must be carefully constructed in multi-threaded applications. If two threads are to execute the creation method at the same time when a singleton does not yet exist, they both must check for an instance of the singleton and then only one should create the new one.

The classic solution to this problem is to use mutual exclusion on the class that indicates that the object is being instantiated.

A Java programming language solution is as follows. It is based on the Q&A link found below, modified for multi-threading, however, it is still vulnerable to the double-checked locking anti-pattern, also found below:

```
public class Singleton {
    private static Singleton INSTANCE = null;

    // Private constructor suppresses
    // default public constructor
    private Singleton() {}

    //synchronized creator to defend against multi-threading
issues
    //another if check here to avoid multiple instantiation
    private synchronized static void createInstance() {
        if (INSTANCE == null) {
            INSTANCE = new Singleton();
        }
    }

    public static Singleton getInstance() {
        if (INSTANCE == null) createInstance();
        return INSTANCE;
```

☞ QUESTION **25**

The command pattern

What is the command pattern? Where is it used?

✍ ANSWER

This is another of the data-driven pattern. The client invokes a particular module using a command. The client passes a request; this request gets propagated as a command. The command request maps to particular modules. According to the command, a module is invoked.

This pattern is different from the Chain of Responsibility in a way that, in the earlier one, the request passes through each of the classes before finding an object that can take the responsibility. The command pattern however finds the particular object according to the command and invokes only that one.

It's like there is a server having a lot of services to be given, and on Demand (or on command), it caters to that service for that particular client.

A classic example of this is a restaurant. A customer goes to restaurant and orders the food according to his/her choice. The waiter/waitress takes the order (command, in this case) and hands it to the cook in the kitchen. The cook can make several types of food and so, he/she prepares the ordered item and hands it over to the waiter/waitress who in turn serves to the customer.

Let's have a look at this example with Java code.

First thing is the Order. The order is made of command which the customer gives the waiter.
Order.java

```java
package bahavioral.command;

/**
 * Order.java
 * This is the command. The customer orders and
 * hands it to the waiter.
 */
public class Order {

private String command;
public Order(String command) {
this.command = command;
}

}// End of class
```

The other thing is the waiter who takes the order and forwards it to the cook.
Waiter.java

```java
package bahavioral.command;
```

```
/**
* A waiter is associated with multiple customers and multiple
orders
*/
public class Waiter {

public Food takeOrder(Customer cust, Order order) {
Cook cook = new Cook();
Food food = cook.prepareOrder(order, this);
return food;
}

}// End of class
```

The waiter calls the prepareFood method of the cook who in turn cooks.
Cook.java

```
package bahavioral.command;

public class Cook {

public Food prepareOrder(Order order, Waiter waiter) {
Food food = getCookedFood(order);
return food;
}

public Food getCookedFood(Order order) {
Food food = new Food(order);
```

return food;

}

}// End of class

Now, here, the waiter takes command and wraps it in an order, the order is associated to a particular customer. For, the cook, the order is associated to a cook and also Food is associated to the Order.

The order is an object which depends on the command. The food item will change as soon as the command changes. This is loose-coupling between the client and the implementation

☞ QUESTION 26

callback function

What is callback function?

✍ ANSWER

Callback function is called by container notify components. It is also called as ejb functions.

☞ QUESTION 27

string and string buffer

What is the difference between string and string buffer?

✍ ANSWER

String objects are immutable. String Buffer supports mutable string. String objects are constants & immutable string Buffer objects are not constants & are growable.

☞ QUESTION 28

final variables inside a method

Can we declare final variables inside a method?

✍ ANSWER

Yes we can declare final variables inside a method.

☞ QUESTION 29

Unicast and Multicast object

What is the exact difference in between Unicast and Multicast object?

Where do we use these?

✍ ANSWER

The following relay some information regarding the question:

The information was taken from (http://saloon.javaranch.com/cgi-bin/ubb/ultimatebb.cgi?ubb=get_topic&f=1&t=000875) written by sasikala kumaresan.

A unicast packet is the complete opposite: one machine is talking to only one other machine. All TCP connections are unicast, since they can only have one destination host for each source host. UDP packets are almost always unicast too, though they can be sent to the broadcast address so that they reach every single machine in some cases.

A multicast packet is from one machine to one or more. The difference between a multicast packet and a broadcast packet is that hosts receiving multicast packets can be on different lans, and that each multicast data-stream is only transmitted between networks once, not once per machine on the remote network. Rather than each machine connecting to a video server, the multicast data is streamed per-network, and multiple machines just listen-in on the multicast data once it's on the network.

☞ QUESTION 30

Java Class and Bean

What is the difference between Java Class and Bean?

✍ ANSWER

A class with no restriction on accessors, mutators or constructors can be considered as a plain Java class. Java Bean is a spl java class with accessors (getters) and mutators (setters) for the instance variables present. Moreover, it can only have a default constructor.

☞ QUESTION 31

Card in Swing

What is the corresponding layout for Card in Swing?

✍ ANSWER

You can use the same card layout in swings also. There is no other layout in swings.

☞ QUESTION 32

components and controllers

What are components and controllers in Java?

✍ ANSWER

Components are the like Frame button. All these are the component of awt package. While controllers are the events whenever we click on any button it is the controller which controls what it has to do.

☞ QUESTION 33

class variables and instance variables

What is class variables and instance variables?

✍ ANSWER

Class variable are class members which are used in the class and instance variable is an object of that class to be used to access methods of the same class.

☞ QUESTION 34

Java Client

What is a "Java Client"?

✍ ANSWER

Java client is a user of those who are developing applications or working with the Java. Meanwhile, Java server is a JVM/ JRE which is running our applications or set of instructions with the business logic.

☞ QUESTION 35

array list and vector

What is the difference between array list and vector?

Which one is more useful? Array list does whatever vector does so why do we need the array list?

✍ ANSWER

Sometimes Vector is better; sometimes Array List is better; sometimes you don't want to use either.

Vector and Array List can both expand size if required. A Vector defaults to doubling the size of its array, while the Array List increases its array size by 50 percent. If you don't know how much data you'll have, you have to know the rate at which it grows. Vector does possess a slight advantage since you can set the increment value.

Basically Vector is synchronized while Array list is not. However, we can make array list also as synchronized by using:

Collections.SyncronizedList(new ArrayList())

☞ QUESTION 36

class level variables

Will class level variables be garbage collected?

✍ ANSWER

No., class level is not GC.

☞ QUESTION 37

JIT and JDK

When does JIT plays its role? Does JIT come along with jdk?
If so then what is the role of interpreter?

✍ ANSWER

JIT - Just in Time compiler, is embedded in the web browser,
like the internet explorer.

The interpreter for Java, which executes the Byte Codes, is the
JVM - Java Virtual Machine.

JIT is also a part of the JVM, and it compiles byte codes into real-
time code, when needed as on demand. The entire Java program
is not compiled into an executable code at once, because there
is a need to perform various run-time checks. However, JIT
compiles code as and when needed, during execution. To put it
simply, the JIT compiler is faster than the JVM.

JIT comes into play when you execute applications written in
JavaScript.

☞ QUESTION **38**

Concept of Pointer

Why is the Concept of Pointer not there in Java?

✍ ANSWER

Pointers are not there mainly to avoid security threats. As JVM restricts access to the file system, thru pointers you can access any memory location. This is the main reason; the other is to avoid the complexity.

☞ QUESTION 39

socket and server socket

What is socket? What is server socket?

✍ ANSWER

Socket is defined as:

socket=port + ip

In layman language socket is liken to where ip is the adress of that fort and port is the gate to enter in to that fort.

Server socket is the socket which is present on the server side. It is basically used to listen to request from clients.

☞ QUESTION 40

current date in jsp

How you can add the 10 days in the current date in jsp?

✍ ANSWER

Date date = new Date();

Calendar cal = new GregorianCalendar();

date=cal.setTime(Calendar.DAYS+10)

date=cal.getTime(date);

☞ QUESTION 41

Tomcat & Weblogic server

Can you give a detailed account on the difference between Tomcat & Weblogic server?

✍ ANSWER

Tomcat is a web-server and Weblogic is an Application Server. In Tomcat we cannot deploy an EJB. However, in Weblogic we can.

☞ QUESTION 42

Main method

Why should main method be declared as public? Why is it that in some versions it is mandatory and in some versions it is not mandatory?

✍ ANSWER

It is because main method is accessed from the outside and it is user oriented.

☞ QUESTION 43

arraylist

Why array list (and other classes) cannot be synchronized?

✍ ANSWER

Array List can not be synchronized because in synchronization the same data at the same time can access with out data loss or data corruption but in Array List it is not possible.

☞ QUESTION **44**

Put semicolon at the end of a class

Why can't we put semicolon at the end of a class in Java?

✍ ANSWER

We can give semicolon at the end of the class but it is not necessary. Generally we will not use that because Java uses } as the end of the class, semicolon for end of the statements.

☞ QUESTION **45**

client server computing

What is client server computing?

✍ ANSWER

Client-Server computing is traditional two-tier architecture. Client "requests" the server for some service or operation, while Server "responds" to the the client with the desired results if the service is available. Client can be a single process or multiple processes on a machine. While server can be single process or multiple process running either on a single or multiple machines.

E.g. of Client/Server:

1) Web browser accessing web pages from a web server.

2) Yahoo messenger accessing Yahoo chat server for chat services.

☞ QUESTION 46

Variable in a class

How can a Variable in a class other than String type are made Immutable.

✐ ANSWER

Provide a constructor to initialize the variable and remove the mutator method (setter method) for that variable.

☞ QUESTION 47

HashMap and TreeMap

Difference between HashMap and TreeMap

✐ ANSWER

HashMap will not store the elements in order. Meanwhile, the TreeMap stores the elements in order. So while retrieving, we will put in a particular order. But for HashMap we won't.

☞ QUESTION 48

☞ **QUESTION 49**

Release an object

How do you release an object which is locked in a synchronized block?

✍ ANSWER

By using notify() or notifyAll() method we can release the lock. But notify() method sometimes notify unwanted thread. So in some situation notify() method is avoidable.

☞ **QUESTION 50**

Enumeration and Iterator

What is the difference between Enumeration and Iterator?

✍ ANSWER

The enumeration interface is what allows you to walk through the elements of a legacy collection(i.e., for Synchronized Collections). Iterator interface is used for stepping through the elements (i.e., for Array List, Linked List).

☞ QUESTION 51

Applet and JApplet

What is the difference between Applet and JApplet?

✍ ANSWER

JApplet is actually a subclass of Applet, so JApplets are in fact Applets in the usual sense. However, JApplets have a lot of extra structure that plain Applets don't have.

☞ QUESTION 52

How operator works

How does operator works?

✍ ANSWER

It is right shift operator, which will produce divide by 2 actions. For example 10>>2 will produce 5. The binary value of 10 is "1010" if we right shift above by one position it will be "0101" this is equivalent to 5.

☞ QUESTION 53

garbage collection

Can we set the time (by user) explicitly for garbage collection?

✍ ANSWER

No, we can't do garbage collection in Java. It is done automatically and programmatically.

☞ QUESTION 54

paint method

What is the disadvantage of paint method in Applet?

✍ ANSWER

The paint() method is called each time a Applet must be redrawn.

☞ QUESTION 55

java.lang Package

Why is the Java language Package the default package?

✍ ANSWER

In java.lang package, object class is the super class of all classes in java language. In order to import that, jdk software implicitly provides the default package.

☞ QUESTION 56

Servelet

What is a servelet?

✍ ANSWER

SERVLETS are the server side applets. These will execute by the server.servlet and does not contain main methods. Servelet having its own life cycle.[init(),service(), destroy()].

☞ QUESTION **57**

JRE and JVM

What is the difference between JRE and JVM?

✍ ANSWER

JRE and JVM both are same. JRE is Java Runtime Environment and JVM is Java Virtual Machine. JRE is defined inside JVM.

☞ QUESTION **58**

servlets and jsp

What is the difference between servlets and jsp?

✍ ANSWER

In servlets, we cannot separate the presentation logic from logic. In jsp we can separate the presentation logic from business logic. In jsp, compilation is done in two stages.

☞ QUESTION 59

servlet cycle

Can we have 3 methods in a single servlet i.e service(), doPost() and doGet() method. If yes, then what method will it be called? What is the servlet cycle in such cases?

✍ ANSWER

First servlet looks for the service() method. If in the case service() method is not present in that appilication, then looks for the doPost() method. If doPost() method is also not present in your appilication ,then servlet looks for the doGet() method. When you used the doGet() method, his method will show to "Querystring" also. It does not provide the security.

☞ QUESTION 60

Platform independent

Is it true the JAVA is really platform independent?

✍ ANSWER

Java is a platform independent but it has some drawbacks. It is not thread independent and garbage collection independent. It is because of that drawback that we are not able to control some real life applications like controlling a plane, controlling a nuclear power station etc.

☞ QUESTION 61

upward and downward casting

What is upward and downward casting in Java?

✍ ANSWER

In upward casting, a small data type is casted into a big data type. One such example is a byte which is casted as int type. In downward casting the big data type is casted into small data type such as a "long data" is casted into int or byte.

☞ QUESTION 62

Clone objects

Where exactly do we make use of Clone objects in a real time?

✍ ANSWER

Clone objects create and return a copy of a particular object. The precise meaning of "copy" may depend on the class of the object. The general intent is that, for any object x, the expression: x.clone() != x will be true, and that the expression: x.clone().getClass() == x.getClass() will be true, but these are not absolute requirements. Copying an object will typically entail creating a new instance of its class, but it also may require copying of internal data structures as well. No constructors are called. The method clone for class Object performs a specific cloning operation. First, if the class of this object does not implement the interface Cloneable, then a Clo neNotSupportedException is thrown. Note that all arrays are considered to implement the interface Cloneable. Otherwise, this method creates a new instance of the class of this object and initializes all its fields with exactly the contents of the corresponding fields of this object, as if by assignment; the contents of the fields are not themselves cloned. Thus, this method performs a "shallow copy" of this object, not a "deep copy" operation. The class Object does not itself implement the interface Cloneable, so calling the clone method on an object whose class is Object will result in throwing an exception at run time. The clone method is implemented by the class Object as a convenient, general utility for subclasses that implement the interface Cloneable, possibly also overriding the clone method, in which case the overriding definition can refer to this utility definition by the call: super. clone() Returns: a clone of this instance. This throws: CloneN otSupportedException - if the object's class does not support the Cloneable interface. Subclasses that override the clone method can also throw this exception to indicate that an instance cannot be cloned. OutOfMemoryError is indicated if there is not enough memory.

☞ QUESTION 63

lock acquisition

Can a lock be acquired on a class?

✍ ANSWER

We can get lock on the class's Class object by using "static synchronize". This is the most exclusive lock.

☞ QUESTION **64**

equals and ==

What is the difference between equals and ==?

✍ ANSWER

The == comparator simply checks to see that two primitives are equivalent by virtue of memory location.

The equals( ) method will actually check to see that the values of the two objects are equivalent.

A good rule of thumb is to always use the equals( ) method when comparing objects and == when comparing primitives.

Example:
```
String h = "Hello";
String h1 = "Hello";
if ( h == h1 )
{
System.out.println( "The two are equal" );
}
else
{
System.out.println( "They are not equal" );
}
```

Of course, they are equal. But now:

```
String h = new String( "Hello" );
String h1 = new String ( "Hello" );
if ( h == h1 )
{
System.out.println( "The two are equal" );
}
else
{
System.out.println( "They are not equal" );
}
```

They are not. You would have to use the .equals( ) method to test for equivalence:

```
if ( h.equals( h1 ) )
```

☞ QUESTION 65

>> and >>> operators

What is the difference between the >> and >>> operators?

✍ ANSWER

The >> operator causes the bits of the left operand to be shifted to the right, based on the value of the right operand. The bits that fill in the shifted left bits have the value of the leftmost bit (before the shift operation).

The >>> operator is identical to the >> operator, except that the bits that fill in the shifted left bits have the value of 0. The >>> operator is said to be an unsigned shift because it does not preserve the sign of the operand.

☞ QUESTION 66

break statement and a continue statement

What is the difference between a break statement and a continue statement?

✍ ANSWER

A statement terminates the current loop iteration and causes execution to break out of a loop.

Meanwhile, a continue statement terminates the current loop iteration and persists the loop with the next iteration.

☞ QUESTION 67

webserver for servlets

What is the webserver used for running the Servlets?

✍ ANSWER

The following servers are available for use of servlets:

1. Tomcat Apache
2. IIS
3. J2ee
4. Jboss
5. BEA WebLogic Server
6. iPlanet
7. Oracle
8. Orion Server
9. WebSphere
10. NetDynamics
11. JRun Server
12. Tomcat
13. JOnAS
14. Pramati Server
15. Power Tier for J2EE

☞ QUESTION 68

multithreading with a single CPU

How does multithreading take place on a computer with a single CPU?

✍ ANSWER

By quickly switching among executing tasks, it creates the impression that the tasks execute simultaneously. If it didn't switch among the tasks, they would execute sequentially.

☞ QUESTION 69

Boolean & operator and the && operator

What is the difference between the Boolean & operator and the && operator?

✍ ANSWER

There is no such thing as a "Boolean &" operator. The & operator is the bitwise-AND operator, and combines two values. It's often used for masking off part of a variable (e.g., to get the two low-order bytes of a 32-bit value, use the expression "value & 0xFFFF").

☞ QUESTION 70

method of the Component class

Which method of the Component class is used to set the position and size of a component?

✍ ANSWER

The method: "setBounds(int x, int y, ing width, int height)".

It is a method of a component to locate and size a component. But it will work **only** when the container doesn't have any one of default **managers**.

If a component **already** has any one of default layouts then the size and **location** of the component is decided by the layout manager.

☞ QUESTION 71

final variable

What is a final variable?

✍ ANSWER

A final variable is the one whose value cannot be changed. It is a constant.

☞ QUESTION 72

generated files

What are the files generated after using IDL to Java Compiler?

✍ ANSWER

My idl file name is My.idl, then when compiled using idlj My.idl the following files will be generated:

My.java
MyHelper.java
MyHolder.java
MyOperations.java
_MyStub.javal

☞ QUESTION 73

layouts in Java

How many layouts are there in Java?

✍ ANSWER

There is a total of 5 layouts in Java?

These are:

1. Flow layout. It is the default layout. It can arrange left to right.
2. Boarder Layout. It can arrange into North, West, South, East order.
3. Card Layout. It follows like a deck of cards (like playing cards).
4. Grid Layout. it can arrange size, and width but there is no guarantee for size and length.
5. Flex Grid Bag Layout. It gives a fix size and length.

☞ QUESTION 74

memory leak

What is meant by memory leak?

✍ ANSWER

Memory leakage occurs due to garbage collection of an object from a list of objects. In case of multithreading, memory leakage occurs during a deadlock.

☞ QUESTION 75

transient variable

What is a transient variable?

✍ ANSWER

Transient instance fields are neither saved nor restored by the standard serialization mechanism. You have to handle restoring them yourself.

☞ QUESTION 76

TextField in a frame

How do you position TextField in a frame so that it would look good and in a manner that the next text field will come in the preceding row?

✍ ANSWER

You can do this with:

gridlayout(no of columns,no.of rows)

set GridLayout(5,2)

When you set your components here, you'll get on the order of 5 x 2.

If you want to put entire things in to order, use: FlowLayout();

☞ QUESTION 77

access modifiers and access specifiers

What is the main difference between access modifiers and access specifiers?

✍ ANSWER

Access Specifiers are private, public, protected and default. Whereas Access modifiers are abstract, static and final.

☞ QUESTION 78

wrapper class

Is String a wrapper class? Explain what a wrapper class is.

✍ ANSWER

No. String is not a wrapper class. Wrapper class is a class that allows us to access primitive data types as objects. There are 8 wrapper classes in Java. These are the Integer, Float, Double, Byte, Character, Short, Long, and Boolean.

☞ QUESTION 79

MVC architecture

Is it necessary that there should be only one controller in MVC architecture? If so, why?

✍ ANSWER

Actually MVC is basically an architecture in which there is clear separation between presentation and business logic.

MVC M(Model) :Is your bean (containing information like name, age, sex, add).

☞ QUESTION 80

multiple inheritance

Why multiple inheritances are not supported through classes in Java?

✍ ANSWER

Java does not support multiple inheritances because:

1. If the two super classes (multiple inheritances contain more than one super class) have the same method, there is confusion in accessing the method;

2. In other hand, in the same scenario, the first super class method alone will be called always.

3. Final and most important reason is, there is chance for code ambiguity.

☞ QUESTION 81

delegation event

What is the difference between Delegation event model and Inheritance event model?

✍ ANSWER

Whether there is any class method in jsp to find from which page the request has come to the current page.

☞ QUESTION 82

range of the short type

What is the range of the short type?

✍ ANSWER

The range is 2 bytes, signed (two's complement), 32,768 to 32,767.

☞ QUESTION 83

null a keyword

Is null a keyword?

✍ ANSWER

According to the Java Language Specification, null, true, and false are technically literal values (sometimes referred to as manifest constants) and not keywords.

☞ QUESTION 84

thread block

Why do thread block on I/O.

✍ ANSWER

Threads block on I/O (that is enters the waiting state) so that other threads may execute while the I/O Operation is performed.

☞ **QUESTION 85**

Vector, Array and Arraylist

What is the difference between Vector, Array and Array List?

✍ **ANSWER**

Below is a list of comparative qualities/characteristics of vector, array and array list:

1. Vector and Array list are grownable or shrinkable whereas array is not.
2. Vector and Array list are implemented from List interface whereas array is a primitive data type;
3. Vector is synchronized where as array list is not; for best performance use array list over vector

☞ QUESTION 86

synchronization

What is synchronization and why is it important?

✍ ANSWER

Synchronization is the way to make our program safe. It is used in multithreading. When we have two or more threads that share a common code there can be some problem like inconsistency of data if one thread is updating data in that code. Thus, if we make that sharable code (common code) synchronized then it ensures that only one thread will be having a right to access that code. Other threads can't access the code until it's free.

☞ QUESTION 87

functionality stubs and skeletons

What are functionality stubs and skeletons?

✍ ANSWER

Stubs are Marshall Arguments that transmits to the server. Skeletons are un-marshaled arguments that pass on to the servant to receive the call for skeleton as a local call.

☞ **QUESTION 88**

stop(), suspend() and resume() methods in JDK 1.2

What's new with the stop(), suspend() and resume() methods in JDK 1.2?

✍ **ANSWER**

While updating Java's version, old methods are deprecated. So, if you ran a program you will receive a deprecated warning in the new version.

With the use of the above mentioned methods, you can compile a run and not encounter problems.

☞ **QUESTION 89**

2 threads communication

How do you connect and let 2 threads communicate with each other?

✍ **ANSWER**

Two thread communicate using the notify, notifyAll and yield methods provided in the Runnable Interface.

☞ **QUESTION 90**

using JDBC

How will you perform a transaction using JDBC?

✍ **ANSWER**

You can perform a transaction by using the auto commit method provided by the connection object.

☞ **QUESTION 91**

garbage collection guarantee

Does garbage collection guarantee that a program will not run out of memory?

✍ **ANSWER**

No it does not. It is because there are objects that are not subject to garbage collection which may cause and consume memory.

☞ **QUESTION 92**

range of the character type

What is the range of the character type?

✐ **ANSWER**

The range of the character type is 0 to $2^{16} - 1$.

☞ **QUESTION 93**

state of a thread

What state does a thread enter when it terminates its processing?

✐ **ANSWER**

When a thread terminates its processing, it enters the dead state.

☞ QUESTION 94

Class path and Import

What is the difference between Class path and Import?

✍ ANSWER

Class path is where you need to specify the path of oracle, and ext. from where these are picked.

Import is used to import the files in your source code.

☞ QUESTION 95

Class.forName and registerDriver()

What is the difference between Class.forName and registerDriver()?

✍ ANSWER

The function registerDriver() registers the JDBC driver with the DriverManager class.

Class.forName() first loads the respective driver into the memory, registers the driver with the Driver Manager class and then creates an instance of the driver to carry out the necessary JDBC actions.

☞ QUESTION 96

anonymous class

What is anonymous class?

✍ ANSWER

Here are the characteristics and definitions of an anonymous class:

1. Anonymous class does not have a name. It can extend a class or implement an interface but cannot do both at the same time.

2. An anonymous class is never abstract.

3. An anonymous class is always an inner class.

4. It is never static.

5. An anonymous class is always implicitly final.

6. Anonymous class is defined in a method that has access to final method variables and also to the outer class's member variables.

☞ QUESTION 97

innerclass

What is innerclass?

✍ ANSWER

An innerclass is enclosed in a class such as:

```
class outer{
}
class inner{
}
```

☞ QUESTION **98**

HTTPServlet and Generic Servlet

What is the difference between the HTTPServlet and Generic Servlet? Explain their methods. What are their parameter names?

✍ ANSWER

Generic Servlet class is a base class that specifies the class structure for protocol independent servlet and acts as a base for different servlets.

HttpServlet is a servlet that extends Generic Servlet and is specialized to work on HTTP protocol.

Generic Servlet has ServletRequest and ServletResponse methods while the HttpServlet has the HttpServletRequest and HttpServletResponse methods.

☞ QUESTION 99

Servelet and the parameters of the service method

What is meant by Servelet? What are the parameters of the service method?

✎ ANSWER

A Servlet is a component that extends the functionality of the server. The service() method of the servlet takes in 2 parameters. These are the HttpServletRequest and the HttpServletResponse objects.

☞ QUESTION 100

parameters in RMI

How will you pass parameters in RMI? Why will you serialize?

✎ ANSWER

Parameter is passed in RMI using Parameter marshalling.

As RMI is used to invoke remote objects, many of the times objects, their references have passed across the network. Hence these objects need to be serialized.

INDEX

Attention SAP Experts

Have you ever considered writing a book in your area of SAP? Equity Press is the leading provider of knowledge products in SAP applications consulting, development, and support. If you have a manuscript or an idea of a manuscript, we'd love to help you get it published!

Please send your manuscript or manuscript ideas to jim@sapcookbook.com – we'll help you turn your dream into a reality.

Or mail your inquiries to:

Equity Press Manuscripts
BOX 706
Riverside, California
92502

Tel (951)788-0810
Fax (951)788-0812

50% Off your next SAPCOOKBOOK order

If you plan of placing an order for 10 or more books from www.sapcookbook.com you qualify for volume discounts. Please send an email to books@sapcookbook.com or phone 951-788-0810 to place your order.

You can also fax your orders to 951-788-0812 .

Interview books are great for cross-training

In the new global economy, the more you know the better. The sharpest consultants are doing everything they can to pick up more than one functional area of SAP. Each of the following Certification Review / Interview Question books provides an excellent starting point for your module learning and investigation. These books get you started like no other book can – by providing you the information that you really need to know, and fast.

SAPCOOKBOOK Interview Questions, Answers, and Explanations

ABAP	-	SAP ABAP Certification Review: SAP ABAP Interview Questions, Answers, and Explanations
SD	-	SAP SD Interview Questions, Answers, and Explanations
Security	-	SAP Security: SAP Security Essentials
HR	-	mySAP HR Interview Questions, Answers, and Explanations: SAP HR Certification Review
BW	-	SAP BW Ultimate Interview Questions, Answers, and Explanations: SAW BW Certification Review
	-	SAP SRM Interview Questions Answers and Explanations
Basis	-	SAP Basis Certification Questions: Basis Interview Questions, Answers, and Explanations
MM	-	SAP MM Certification and Interview Questions: SAP MM Interview Questions, Answers, and Explanations

SAP BW Ultimate Interview Questions, Answers, and Explanations

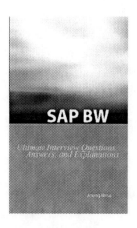

Key Topics Include:

- The most important BW settings to know
- BW tables and transaction code quick references
- Certification Examination Questions
- Extraction, Modeling and Configuration
- Transformations and Administration
- Performance Tuning, Tips & Tricks, and FAQ
- Everything a BW resource needs to know before an interview

mySAP HR Interview Questions, Answers, and Explanations

Key topics include:

- The most important HR settings to know
- mySAP HR Administration tables and transaction code quick references
- SAP HR Certification Examination Questions
- Org plan, Compensation, Year End, Wages, and Taxes
- User Management, Transport System, Patches, and Upgrades
- Benefits, Holidays, Payroll, and Infotypes
- Everything an HR resource needs to know before an interview

SAP SRM Interview Questions, Answers, and Explanations

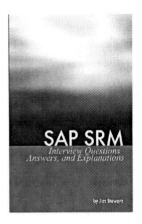

Key Topics Include:

- The most important SRM Configuration to know
- Common EBP Implementation Scenarios
- Purchasing Document Approval Processes
- Supplier Self Registration and Self Service (SUS)
- Live Auctions and Bidding Engine, RFX Processes (LAC)
- Details for Business Intelligence and Spend Analysis
- EBP Technical and Troubleshooting Information

SAP MM Interview Questions, Answers, and Explanations

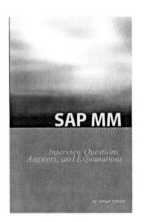

- The most important MM Configuration to know
- Common MM Implementation Scenarios
- MM Certification Exam Questions
- Consumption Based Planning
- Warehouse Management
- Material Master Creation and Planning
- Purchasing Document Inforecords

SAP SD Interview Questions, Answers, and Explanations

- The most important SD settings to know
- SAP SD administration tables and transaction code quick references
- SAP SD Certification Examination Questions
- Sales Organization and Document Flow Introduction
- Partner Procedures, Backorder Processing, Sales BOM
- Backorder Processing, Third Party Ordering, Rebates and Refunds
- Everything an SD resource needs to know before an interview

SAP Basis Interview Questions, Answers, and Explanations

- The most important Basis settings to know
- Basis Administration tables and transaction code quick references
- Certification Examination Questions
- Oracle database, UNIX, and MS Windows Technical Information
- User Management, Transport System, Patches, and Upgrades
- Backup and Restore, Archiving, Disaster Recover, and Security
- Everything a Basis resource needs to know before an interview

SAP Security Essentials

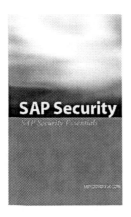

- Finding Audit Critical Combinations
- Authentication, Transaction Logging, and Passwords
- Roles, Profiles, and User Management
- ITAR, DCAA, DCMA, and Audit Requirements
- The most important security settings to know
- Security Tuning, Tips & Tricks, and FAQ
- Transaction code list and table name references

SAP Workflow Interview Questions, Answers, and Explanations

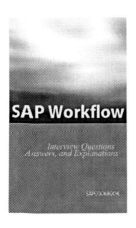

- Database Updates and Changing the Standard
- List Processing, Internal Tables, and ALV Grid Control
- Dialog Programming, ABAP Objects
- Data Transfer, Basis Administration
- ABAP Development reference updated for 2006!
- Everything an ABAP resource needs to know before an interview

Printed in the United States
106100LV00001B/342/A